# Hello,

I am a trainer with professional education and work experience of 15 years, **FIDE** master.
My students are winners of the Moscow Regional Competitions, as well as the tournament in Boston.
In addition, other disciplines were studied and taught to preschoolers, in particular reading, early development, preparation for school.
And I know how important it is to develop a child comprehensively.
This book is not only a unique and only interactive tutorial on chess, but also an excellent assistant in preparing a child for school, because it contains tasks for logic, imagination, preparing your hands for writing, and chess itself easily develop all these qualities in playful and natural way.
The book includes educational, instructive stories about a kitty and his friends, which makes it even more attractive to a young reader. The content of the book is quite deep: from the names of the pieces to solving problems and analyzing chess games. This book will be a great friend and helper for your child!
Be sure to visit our site with copyright books and manuals
www.magicchessworld.com

Yours respectfully, Z. Bondarenko.

# ACQUAINTANCE WITH CHESS KINGDOM

**Lesson 1**

Hello, you see two troops in front of you: black and white.
And each of them is ruled by the king, as in a real state.
Finding it is very easy! Let's find the biggest, largest piece of white.

and now black

Let's take it in the hands and say loudly:
**«KING»**
And raise it higher than all the other pieces.

But you know that it's very difficult to manage such a large state,
and therefore the king needs an assistant,
he stands next to the king - Queen.

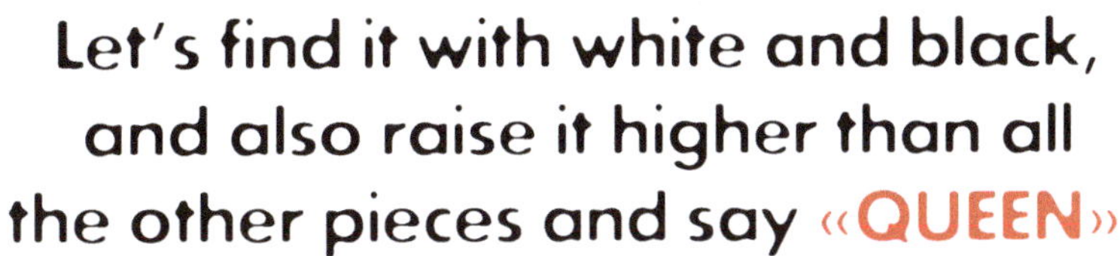

Let's find it with white and black,
and also raise it higher than all
the other pieces and say «QUEEN».

On the sides of the king
and queen are their younger
helpers – «BISHOPS»,
2 for white and 2 for black.

Knights live next to bishops
in our kingdom, you can easily find
them and you can show
black and white: «KNIGHTS!»

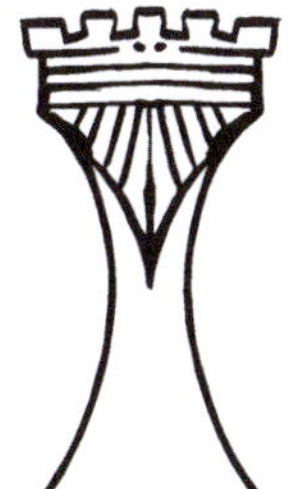

In the corners of our chessboard are rooks.
Let's show one: «ROOK!»
And the second: «ROOK!»
And opposite we will find black rooks

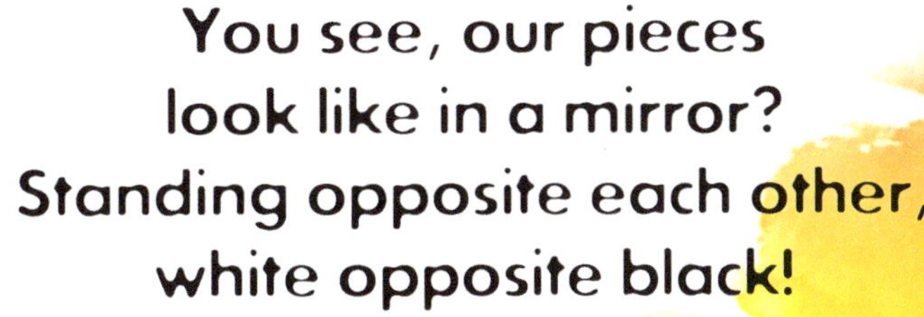

You see, our pieces
look like in a mirror?
Standing opposite each other,
white opposite black!

And now we have to get acquainted with the smallest
and most brave warriors on a chessboard - pawns.
They are like soldiers: small and brave, all the same.

Let's count them!

Now let's count with black?
Suddenly they have more?


Who has more?
CORRECTLY, NO ONE, EVERYONE IS EQUAL.
Well, here we are and met with the whole chess troop.

**And now we have to get acquainted with the black and white chess country. It is called a «chessboard».**

<table>
<tr><td>8</td><td colspan="8"></td></tr>
<tr><td>7</td><td colspan="8"></td></tr>
<tr><td>6</td><td colspan="8"></td></tr>
<tr><td>5</td><td colspan="8"></td></tr>
<tr><td>4</td><td colspan="8"></td></tr>
<tr><td>3</td><td colspan="8"></td></tr>
<tr><td>2</td><td colspan="8"></td></tr>
<tr><td>1</td><td colspan="8"></td></tr>
<tr><td></td><td>A</td><td>B</td><td>C</td><td>D</td><td>E</td><td>F</td><td>G</td><td>H</td></tr>
</table>

**Color the chess country yourself!**

These are the streets and houses of our pieces. Let's remove the pieces from the board: you're white, I'm black (can be on the contrary). And continue. Who will remove the pieces faster: you or me? Well, here is our beautiful black and white country! There are streets on it - these are lines and house numbers - these are the numbers that you see from the side.

# But first, we will check: how does the rook move?

Let's put it in a corner and try to move it forward as far as it can or as much as you want. But strictly in a straight line!

Well done, but now you can go down a little or run to the side: left or right. Where do you want? Let's try it in all directions?

But it is important to let go of your hand after each move. Otherwise, the move will not be completed. **THIS RULE IS!**

While we are watching moves for pieces of the same color, but in chess everyone moves in turn and later I will show you this!

# Now say:
# do you like to eat?

And what is your favorite dish?
- Dumplings!
Pizza, ice cream, sweets! …
- Excellent, and you know,
our rook also likes to eat?

It only eats delicious chess pieces!
It can eat a whole plate! It likes to eat the queen,
the bishop, the rook, the knight, and the pawns.

All except the king.
Kings are never eaten.
Under no circumstances.
It is too important, they just catch king,
so as it can't to run away.
So, let's try to eat the pieces. In order
to take / capture a piece, you need
to stand with it on the same line
along which the rook goes,
this will be an attack.

And after the attack, we can take whoever we want (provided
that our move) is now our move, and we capture, for example,
a delicious queen and you can stroke your tummy and rook at
the same time.
SO TASTY!

# ROOK CHECK

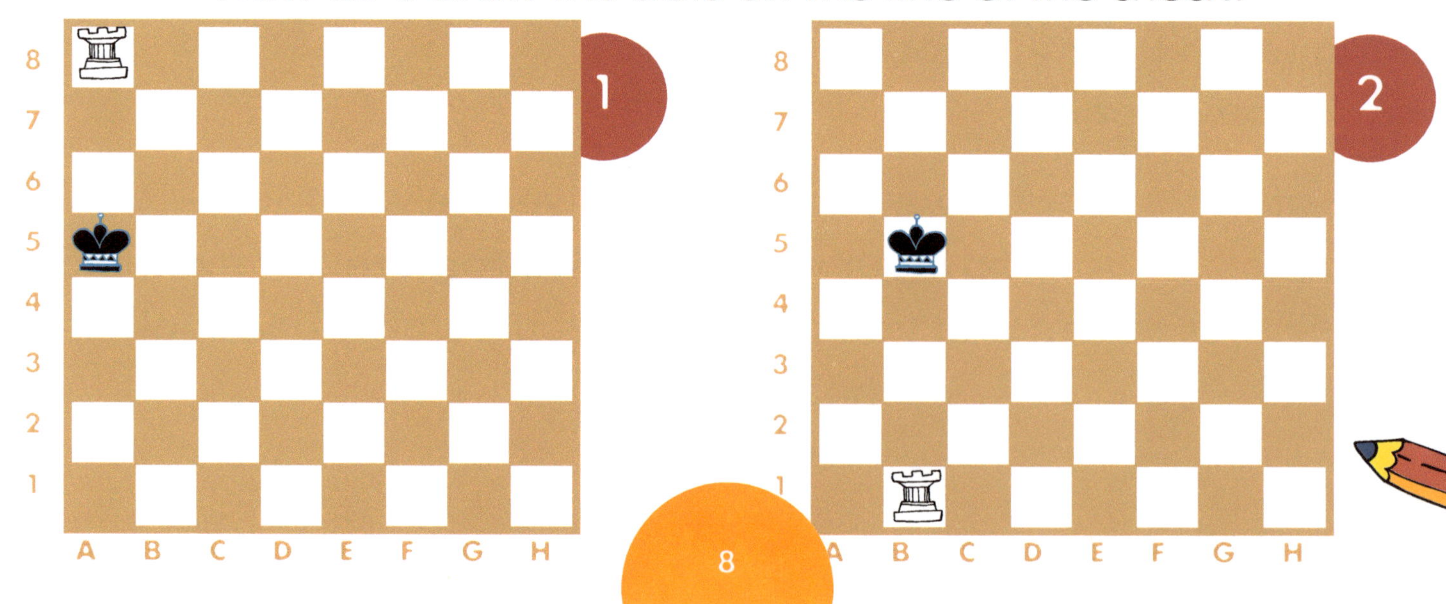

## ROOK CHECK — PRACTICAL WORK

Now let's draw the dots on the line of the check.

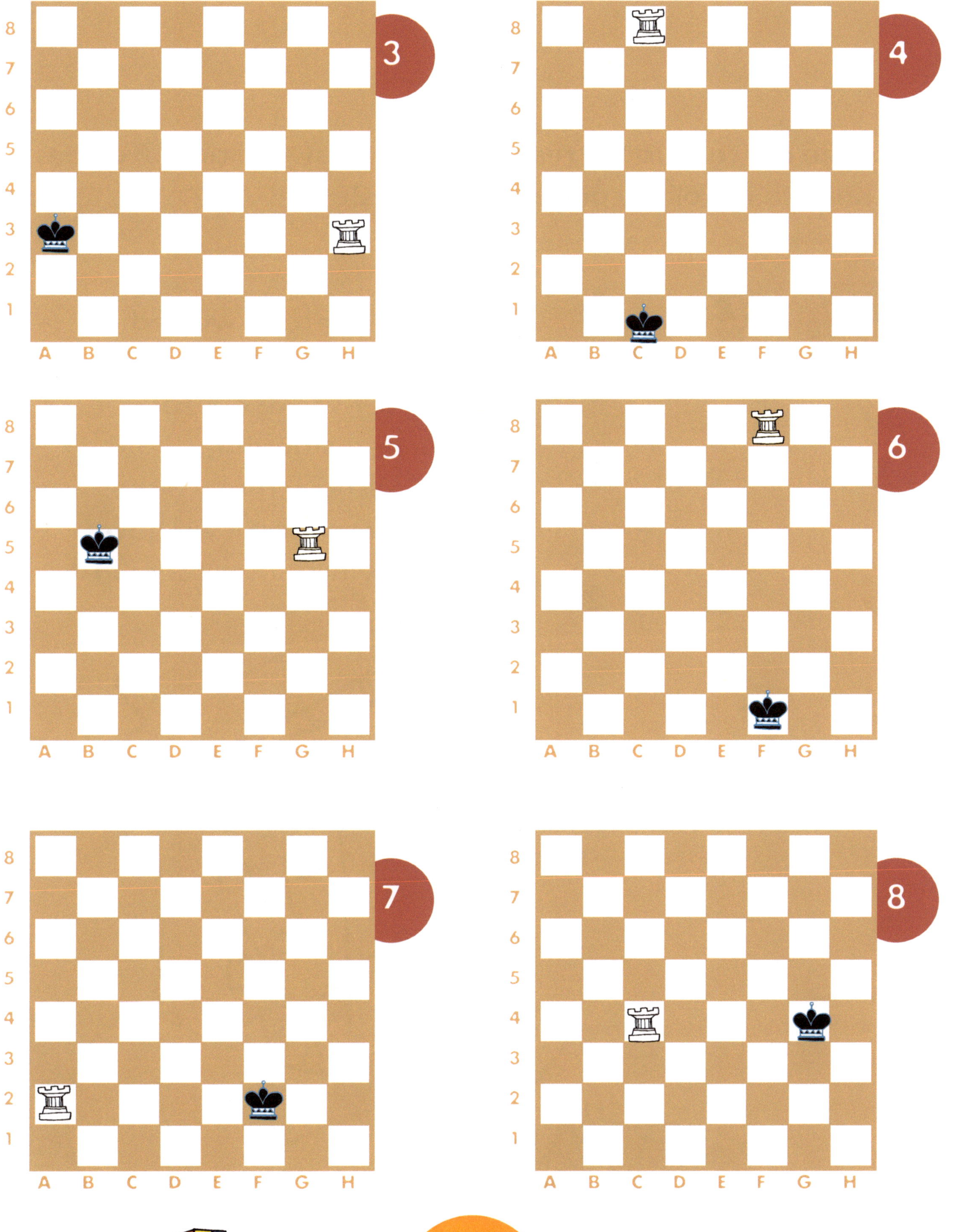

# «RESTAURANT FOR ROOK»

We invite our rook to the restaurant, see how delicious it awaits!
You need to eat all the pieces in 8 moves!

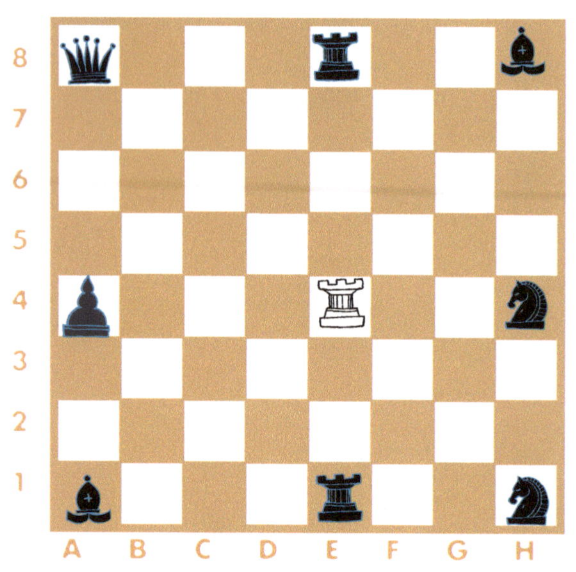

You know, our rook walked
a lot today and walked up a good
appetite! Let's take our rook
in a cafe or restaurant,
where it will have many dishes
to choose from and it will have
to eat everything that it sees in its
path.

Well done! You did a great job!
And your rook is not hungry now!
It has a full belly.

# KING



The king is the most important, but the weakest.
That's because it is just old and therefore can only move
one square in any direction!
Let's practice with you!

We have one king white and the other black.
And then one day they decided to visit each other.
Now let's play with two kings!
Our kings are very fond of drinking tea, and sometimes even
coffee, and once they went to visit each other,
and we will show you how it was!

Our kings are visiting each other!
Rushing to tea with cake and delicious sweets.
Who is quicker?
White makes the first move!
We put the kings in different
corners of the chessboard
on the 1st and 8th rank
and begin to move,
remembering the sequence
of moves along the way.

But our kings did not know
that the other king
went on a visit without warning,
and did not find each other
at home.

Upset, offended and quarreled.

**Whose king came before?**
**Why do you think?**

And do you think our kings are
friends or not?
That's right, they are not friends,
because they are rulers of different
states and they just have different rules
of life. And they remember their
offences when they went to visit
and no one was at home.
Since then, our kings are not friends,
which means that

**they do not stand nearby.**

**Show how the king move**

They don't drink
coffee together.

Now let's repeat it:

**«Two kings don't stand nearby!»**

You know this rule,
let's try playing with kings again.
But this time I will put them
opposite each other.
Each king moves to visit again,
and at a meeting they
should not collide!

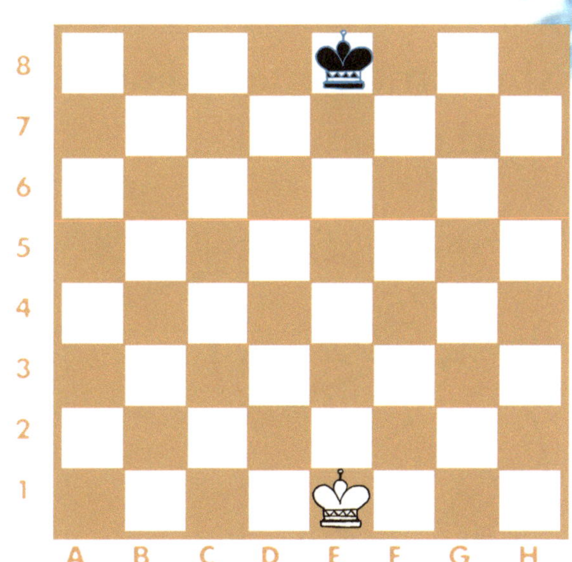



**So white are bold
and they make the first move!**

# QUEEN

**Lesson 3**

Hello,
today I will introduce you
to the strongest piece on the board.
This queen is the king's main assistant and adviser.

The queen moves the same way
as the king, but it is younger,
so moves further.
Queen moves as far as it can see.
It's maybe straight lines,
or maybe diagonal.
But before we begin
to move the queen, I will offer
to show me straight lines
up and down – files .

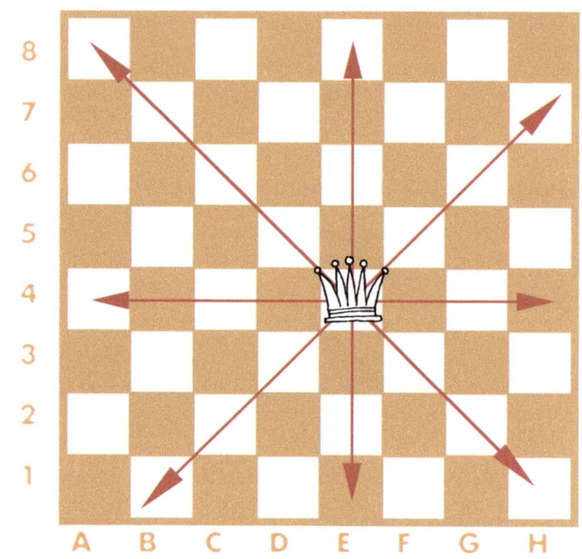

Let's run a hand over them.
What straight lines do you like?
And now to the side,
from left to right and from right to left.
These lines are called rankes.
And we also have unusual lines that
are connected together by corners
and these are lines of the same color.

We call them diagonals.

14

Now we'll practice showing them, and then you can lay them
out, for example, with magnets or pawns of the same color, and
we can draw with you!

Do you like drawing?!
Look what I've got! I have such
an interesting chessboard
and we will mark the queen's
moves with dots or lines.
Happened? Fine.
Now take the queen and put it
on the board. Trying to walk?
Well done! You are doing great!

And a little bit, I'll tell you today about the queen's check.

The queen places the check also. It likes walking.
Files, ranks and diagonals.
If it is on the same line with the king, then the king is «check».

A check is when a piece attacks the king,
and it is obliged to hide from the check or run away..

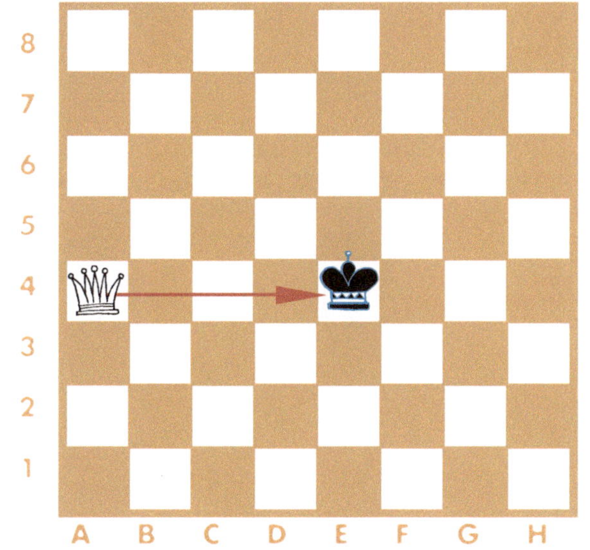

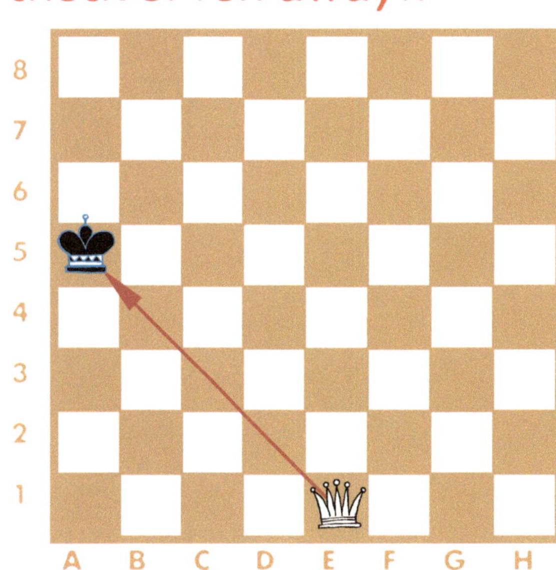

Practice it?

Circle the queen's check.

Find where the word is hidden

circle and color the names of the pieces

adfbghjkfkingyrkixml
hffvhrireieoknightnsgtsesrookser
mrewihfiehpawnhwerkh
adthgtsrkoqueenhriuewkwiug

# BISHOPS

Hello.
Our lesson today
will be with bishops.

Two bishops are little brothers,
In black-and-white little coats,
They all run along the path,
On white-there, on black-here!
Let's show them!

Well done! Now take them in your hands and put them on the chessboard: one on a white square, the other on a black one. And now I will tell you that bishops like to move very much, but they move not just like that, but along special paths, which are called diagonals. Diagonal lines of the same color, interconnected by corners.

So let's try it. Let's see: there are long diagonals, there are very short ones, consisting of only 2 squares. Let's find the longest diagonal of white color and count: how many squares are there in it? 1,2,3,4,5,6,7,8. Right, 8!
Now we find such a diagonal in black.

# Well done, let's count again?

## 1,2,3,4,5,6,7,8.

### Great for you!

Let's move bishop
on one of the diagonals?
A bishop that stands on
a white square is a white-squared,
a bishop that stands
on a black square is
a black-squared.
Well done.

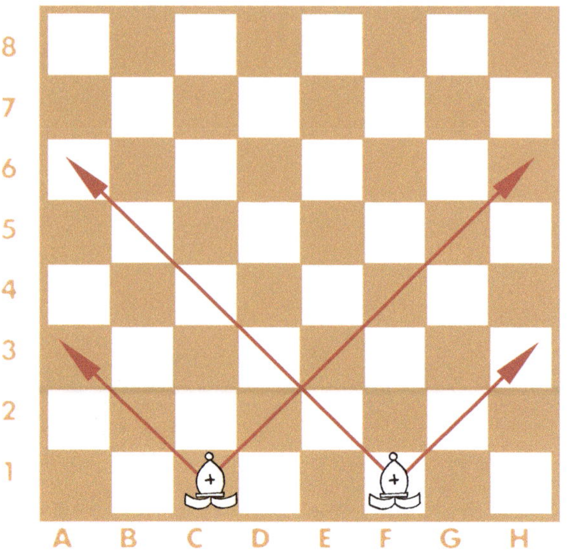

And now let's go feed them delicious,
for example, pawns or knights?
Or maybe the queen and the rooks?
What do your bishops love?
And now we'll try to do the same
in the picture using dots!
Dot the path of the bishop!

Fine.
Now draw the line of the check yourself.

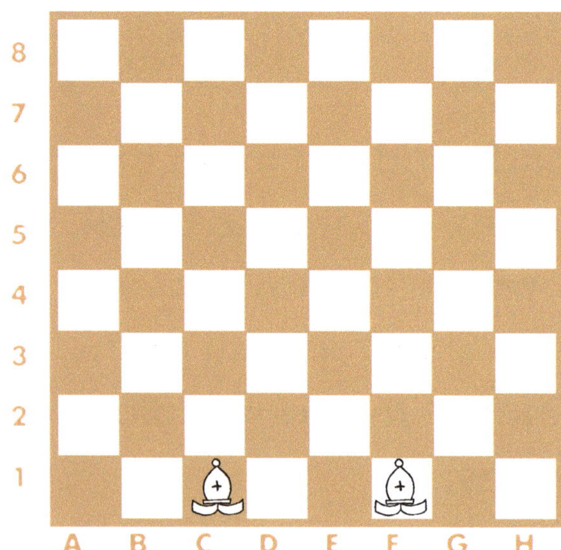

## Check by bishop

## That's all for today! I will be glad to see you again!

# PAWN

**Lesson 5**

Pawns are little soldiers, the bravest ones on the chessboard. This is a special squad. A pawn walks in a straight line for one move. And just go! A pawn can jump the first move through the square, or it can make a move on only one square.

Let's try?
Top-top-top …

And reached the end!
What now?

Now we will see:
if the pawn has a long way or no?
Yes, it was long, it tried very hard
to reach the end and for this
 it is entitled to an amazing reward!
It can become any piece except the king!
What pieces do we know?
That's right: queen, bishop,
knight, rook. I will tell you a secret.
Most often, a pawn turns into
a queen, because it is the strongest!
But there are exceptions.
So, we change the pawn
to the queen!
Wow!

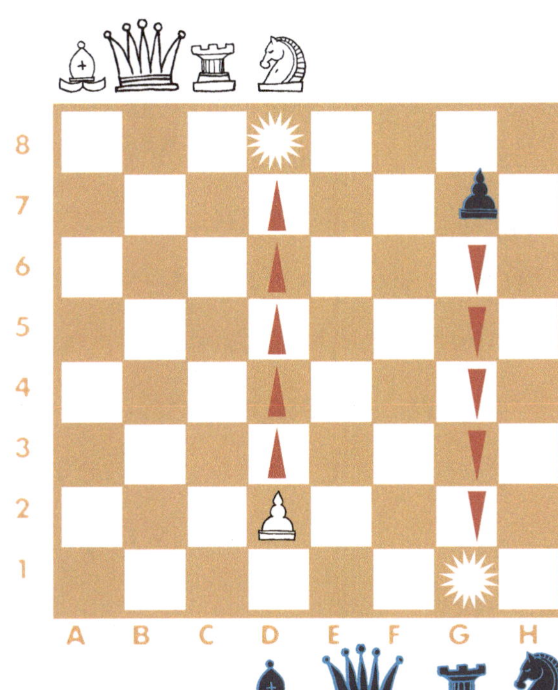

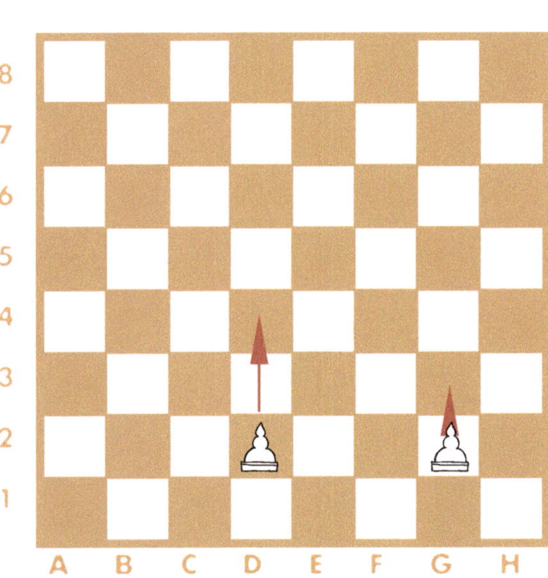

Now let's revise and I will tell you something else interesting about the pawn! It is very, very brave, so it can jump the first move! Imagine how a frog! Jump!
And then again, in one small move.

There is one rule: that a pawn can only jump this way if this move is the first in its small pawn's life.
If this is not so, then it can only do one move.

This is a rule!
And now let's move: someone who turns the pawn into a queen will be the winner! Which pawn do you want to play: black or white?
We put pawns on h2 and a7.
Let's remember who starts in chess first: white or black? That's right, white. White are bold. Getting started. Which pawn came first? Right, white, and what do you think: why? Yes, because white started earlier, well done! Now look at the position: the queen «looks» at the queen and your move! What can we do? That's right, «eat» it. Oh, how delicious!

**Check pawn**

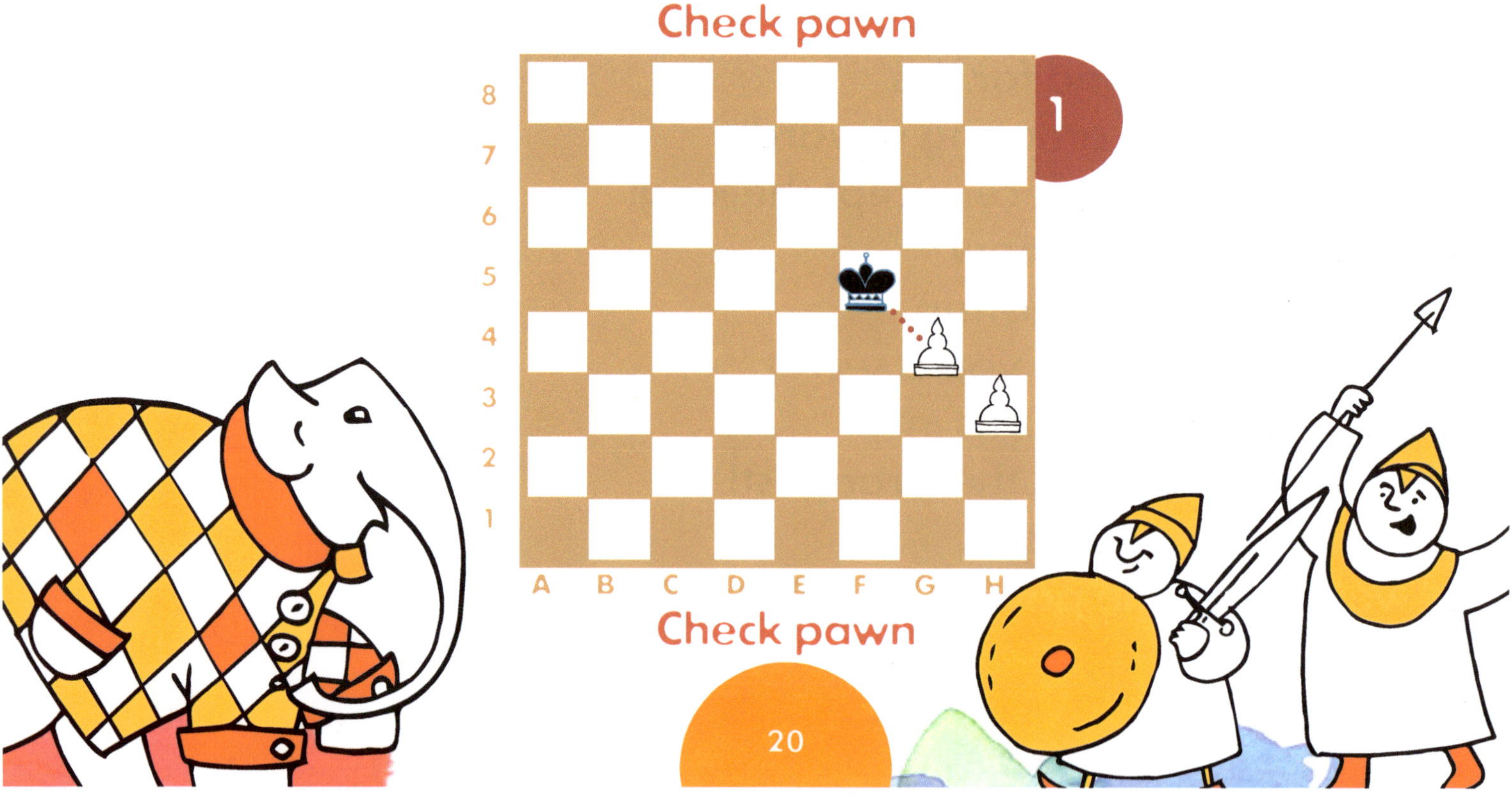

**Check pawn**

20

# PAWN, CAPTURE

## Lesson 6

Hello,
today we will revise the lesson
about how a pawn moves
and then I will tell you how it beats

So, let's start.
The game of pawns on
the distillation as
in the previous lesson.
Well done, remember everything,
and now with a little complication.
So, your pawn has reached the end
and again became the queen,
as before!
And let's see what has changed?
That's right, it's check to king!

Now, according to the chess rules, the king must leave. It can't stand there! It left and now you can beat …? Whom? That's right, queen! Well done?
Did you like it?


White begin.
Well done, you and I played!
Wow!

Our «hungry» pawn eats
diagonally one square.
Both to the right and to the left.
Depending on where
the enemy snacks
are or what piece
to beat is «tastier».

Come on, practice.

That's all for today. 

# REPETITION

Today we will revise again how the pawn moves, how it beats,
and I will tell you something interesting about it! Look!
I will tell you about the «fork».
This is when our pawn was lucky enough to attack 2 opponent's
pieces at once, for example, a rook and a knight: You see, a
pawn can beat a knight or a rook?

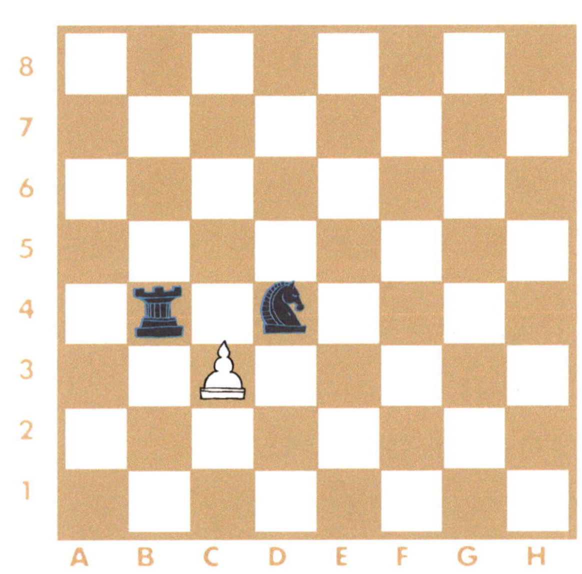

For example, now the black's move
and the rook are running
now we will practice with you.
We make several similar positions.

And now you already know how
a pawn moves, beats, turns and
even puts forks! And I propose
to fight with our soldiers:
who will turn faster?

Let's guess: in which hand I hid the pawn, what color do you
guess, so you will play! Hooray, you got a white color!
White begin. We only consider pawns without pieces
and play (at first, you must give in strongly
and show possible eating pawns).
So we play a couple of times.

Today our lesson is over.
And next lesson I will show you how a knight moves.

# KNIGHT

A knight moves with the letter «L».
And you can also say: «jump-jump and sideways»
or «side-jump-jump»!

You can jump in any direction!
Let's try it, get started, well done.
We train and jump up, down,
to the sides. And now we will travel
with a knight eating something tasty,
for example, pawns,
they will be like sweets with tea!
Well done, can we try
to bring down the queen?
Well done! Tasty!

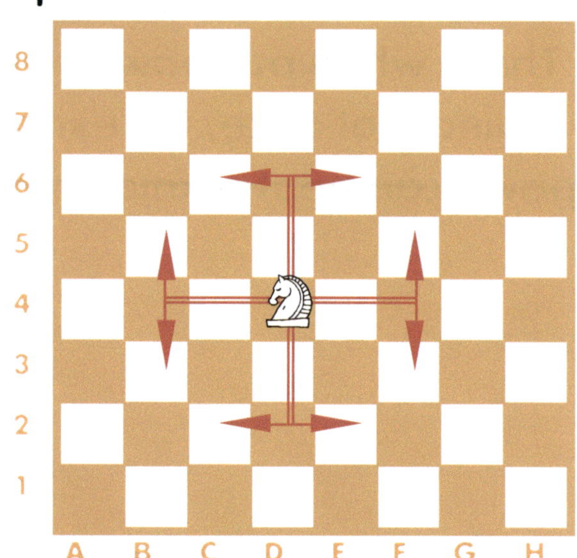

And now our white knight gallops
to black. We put 2 knights
on the squares A1 and H8
and look for a suitable route!
After the position is changed
to knights standing on A8 and H1.

Then black knight goes to visit white
from these positions.
Wow. Work out!
Now you know how all the pieces
on the chessboard move!

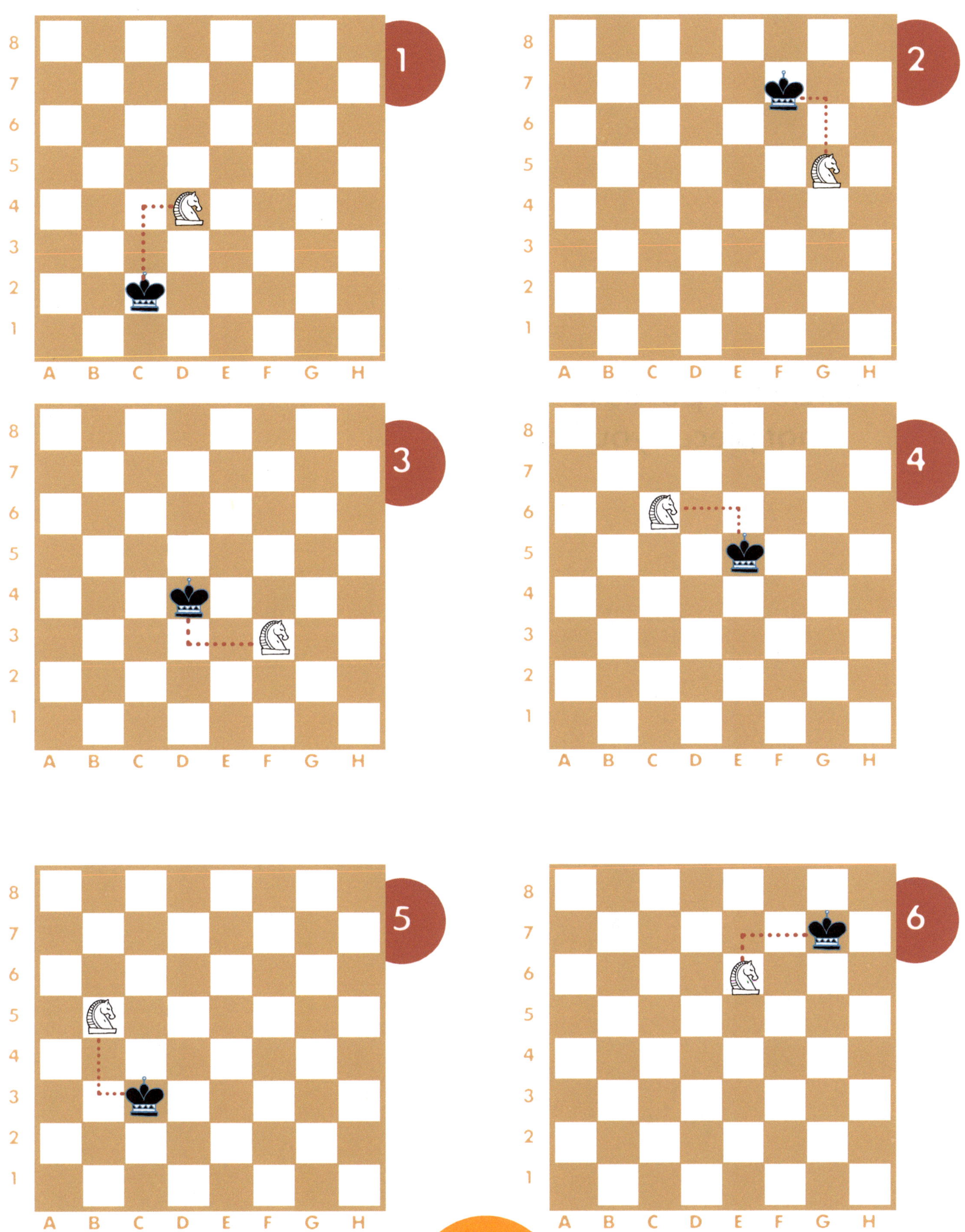

Circle the points to see
what pieces you have

# CHECK WITH KNIGHT

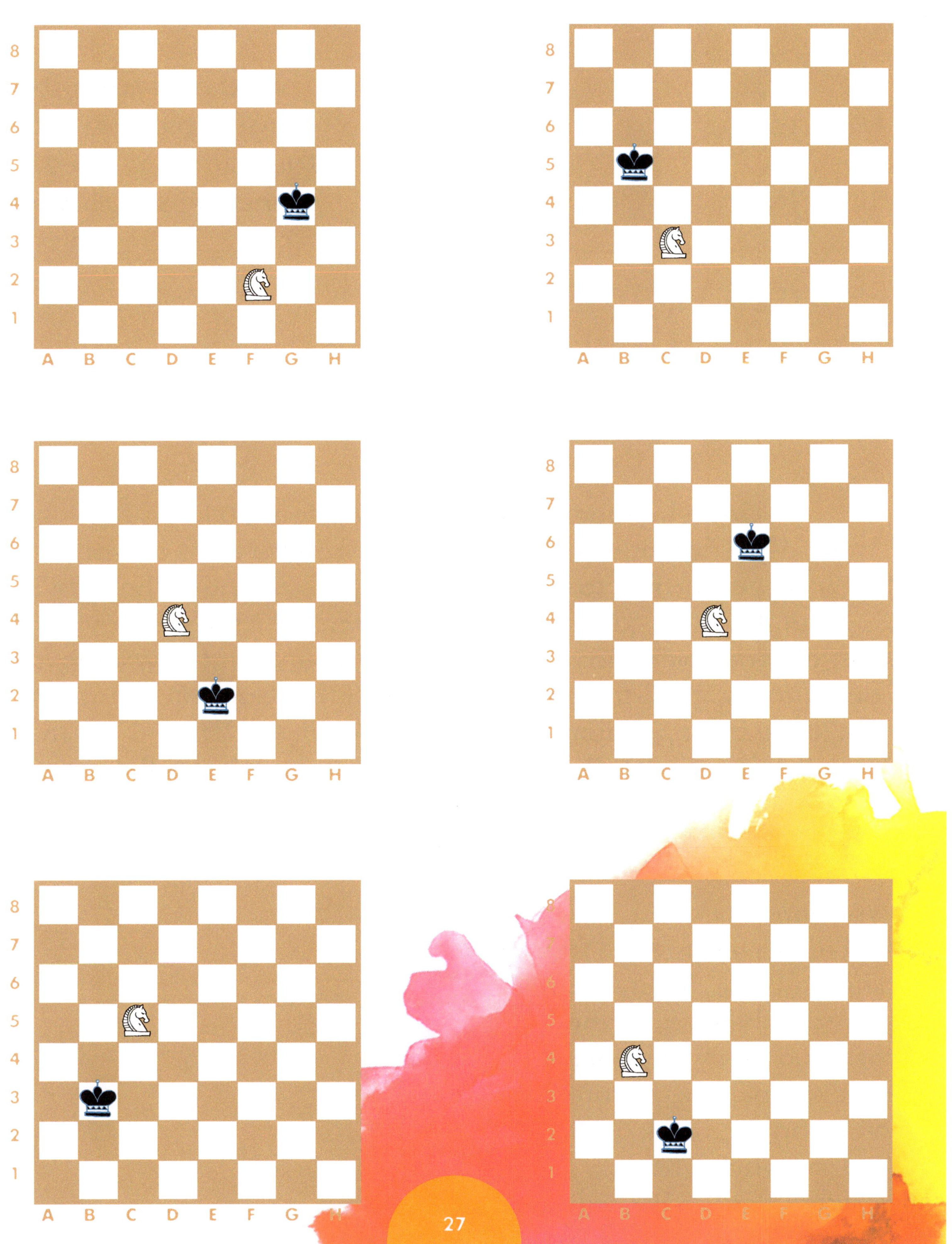

now try to draw the line of the check yourself



# CHECK, CHECKMATE, RULES

So, remember that we have 2 offended kings
who are not friends with each other and they are at war.
Our pieces according to the rules of kings do not have the right to
beat. But they can be attacked. And now I'll tell you how.
After all, each piece has its own way of moving and how it moves
and attacks, everything is very simple! If the rook is in a straight
line, if the bishop is diagonally, if the knight, the letter «L», if the
king, then around it. Only a pawn is different. It beats the pieces
in the same way as attacks! Will we try?
Within 15 minutes we try to set the check with various pieces.

Well done!
And now I will give the task more
difficult. Look. Today we will try
to attack the king, so that it
can't run away anywhere.
For example: there were 2 kings.
White on A6, black on A8.
And the white king
had a rook on H1.



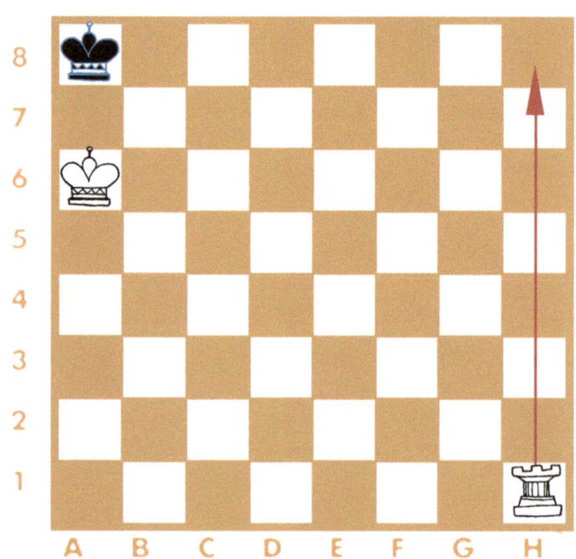

You and I need to put the rook check to the black king.
How? That's right, R H1-H8. Now let's see if the king can go
down? No, who gets it? That's right, under the king!
It's impossible, because we remember the rule that
«the white king and the black king are not near»?!
Well, it turns out that the king has nowhere to move?
This situation, when the king can't be saved from the attack,
is called «checkmate». That is a «checkmate» is a «check» from
which there is nowhere to hide (leave or close with another piece,
or beat a piece who puts a checkmate).
Let's try?
We train on simple checkmates. In one move.

# PRACTICUM-1.

## Little tasks.



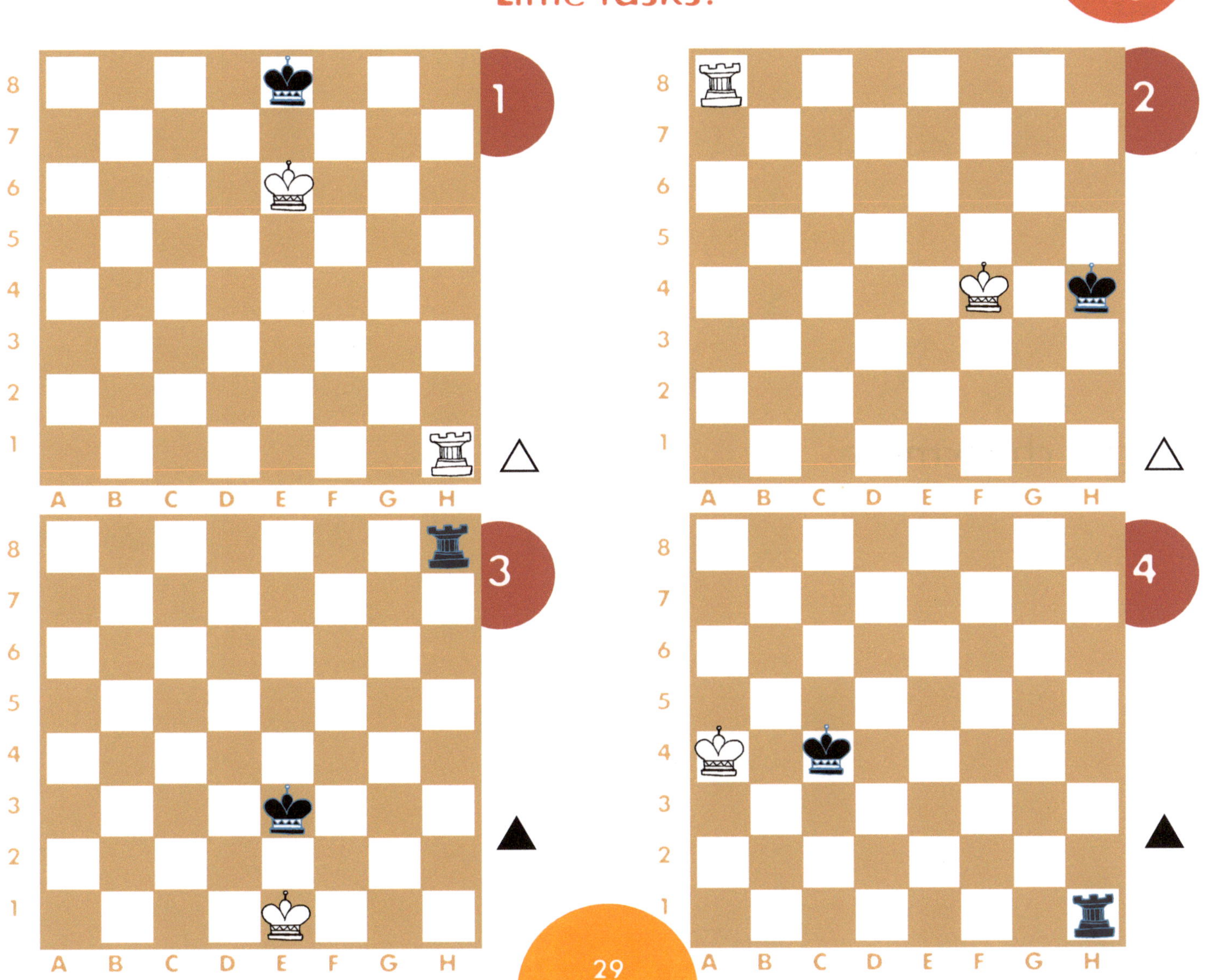

# Line checkmate:

# Knight checkmate:

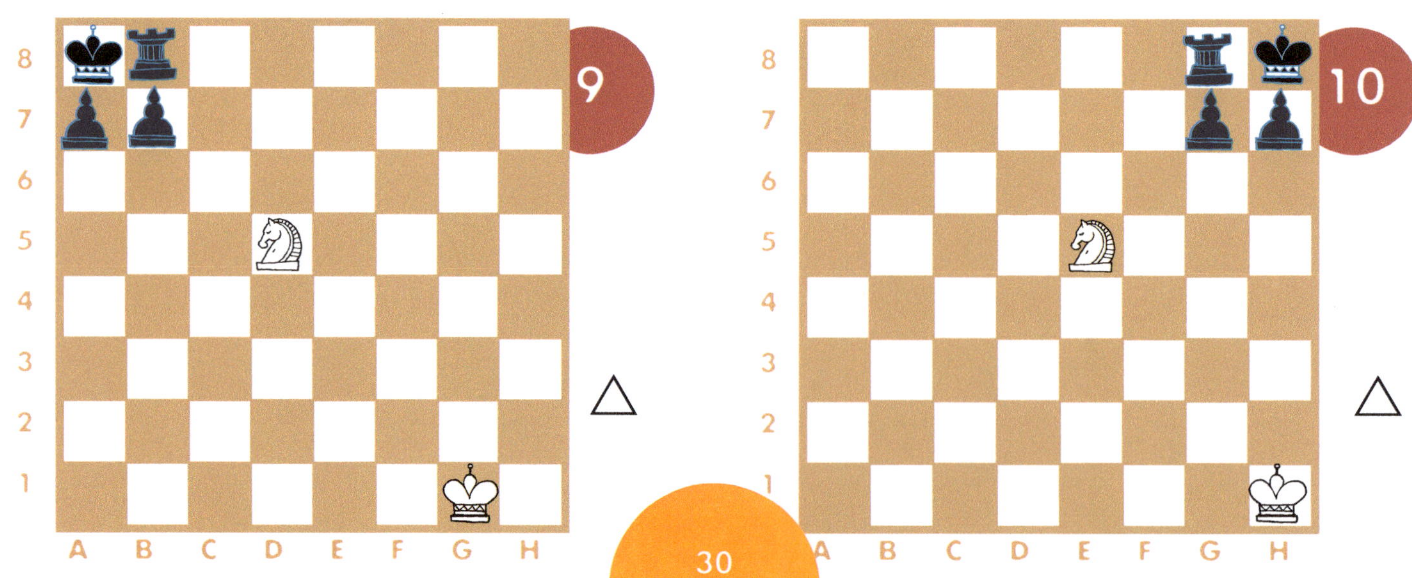

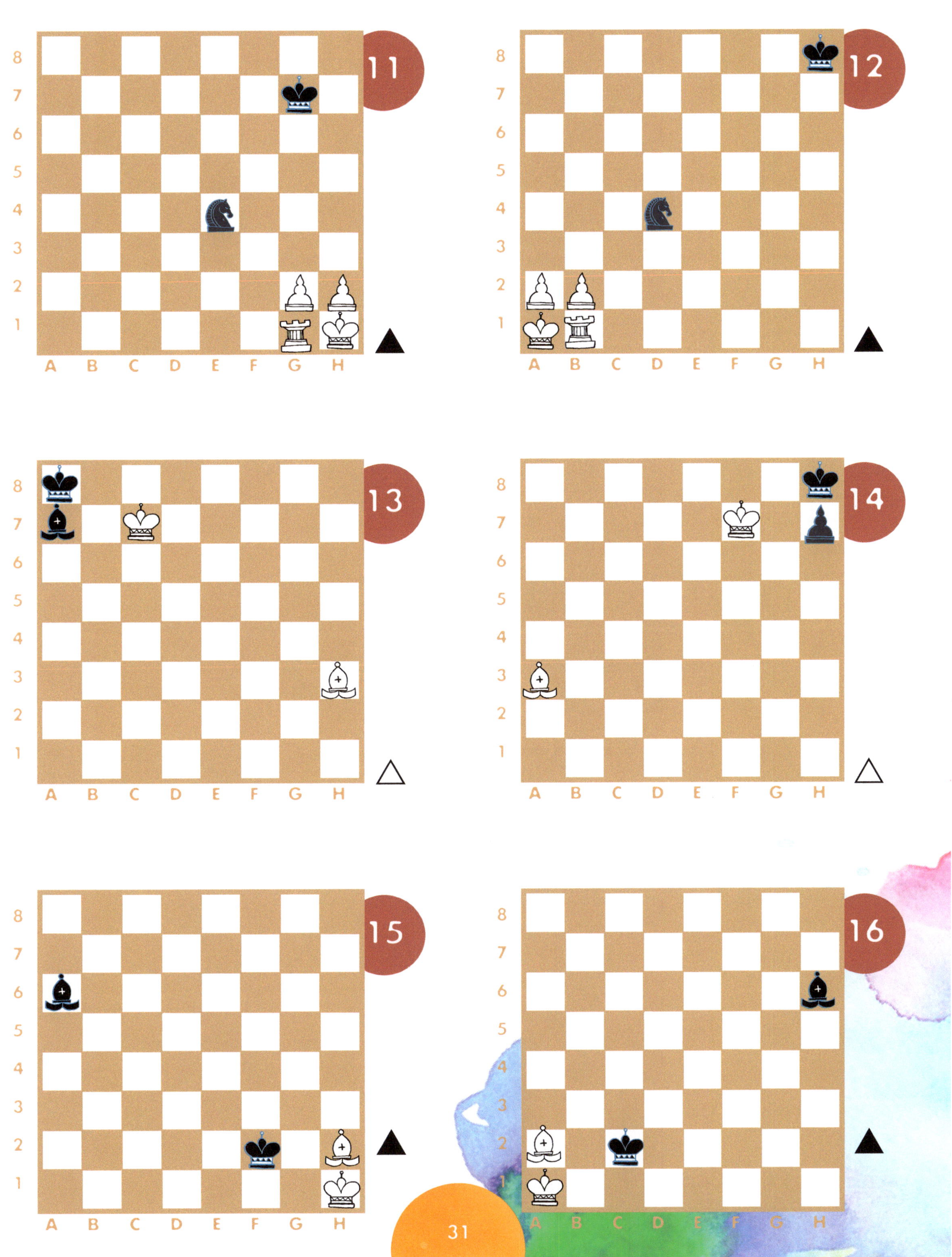

# Pawn checkmate in 1 move:

## Pawn checkmate in 1 move:

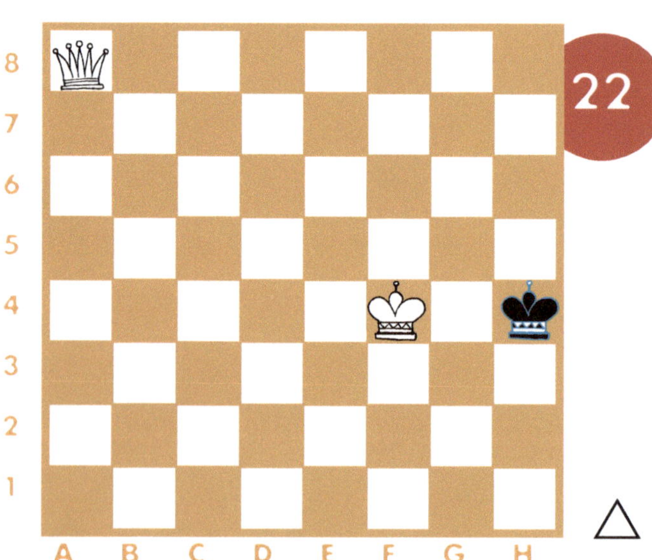

You can find answers on page 41

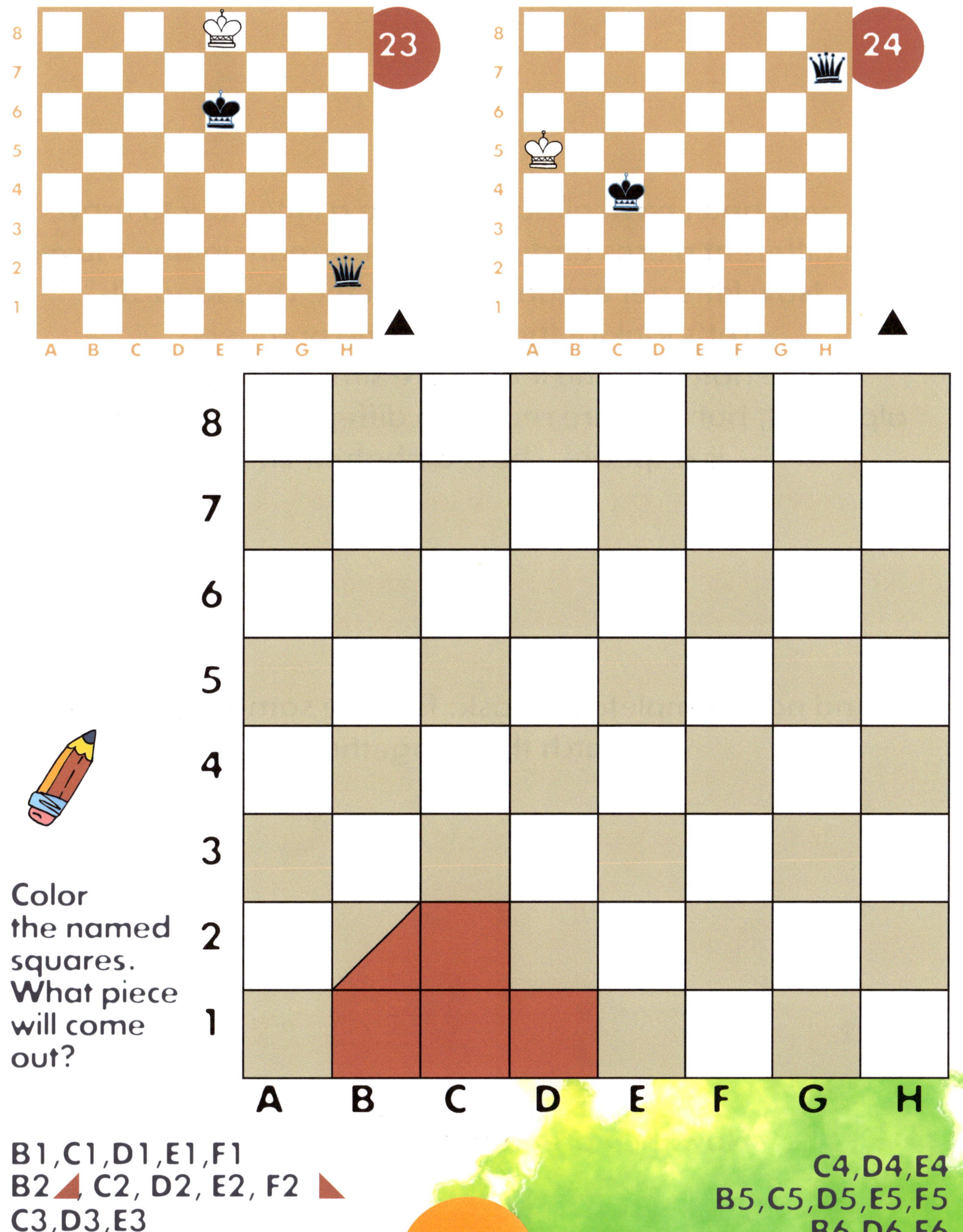

23

24

Color the named squares. What piece will come out?

B1,C1,D1,E1,F1
B2, C2, D2, E2, F2
C3,D3,E3

C4,D4,E4
B5,C5,D5,E5,F5
B6,D6,F6

33

# LETTERS AND NUMBERS

So, you and I have already known a little how to move with different pieces and put the checkmate in one move. Now let's get acquainted with the chessboard!
Let's look at the letters and numbers!
Please note that the letters are similar to the English alphabet, but they are read in a different way, because it is a special, chess alphabet, Latin.
Remember! A (a), B (be), C (ce), D (de), E (e), F (ef), G (ge), H (ash). So we move from the letter «A» to the letter «H» (ash)! Repeat! And now we go back from the guests from the letter «H» (ash) to the letter «A».

And now complete the task: find the same letters and match them together!

That's it, twin brothers.
Now they are together and hugging.
Hooray!

# FILES AND RANKS

Well, well, I'll tell you now that our letters indicate the lines on the chessboard – file – a row of squares located from bottom to top.

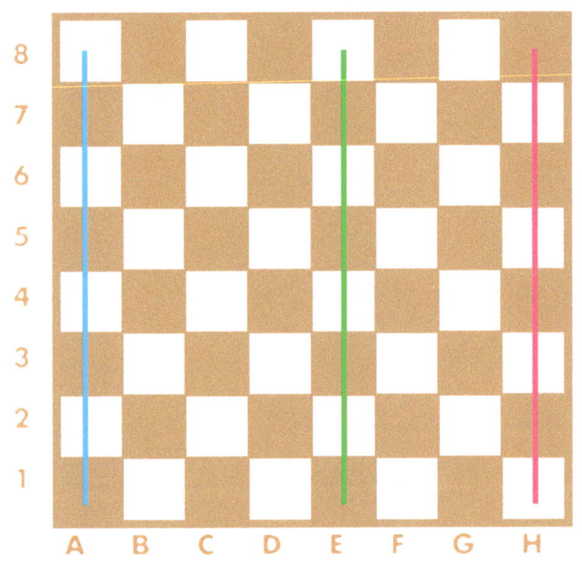

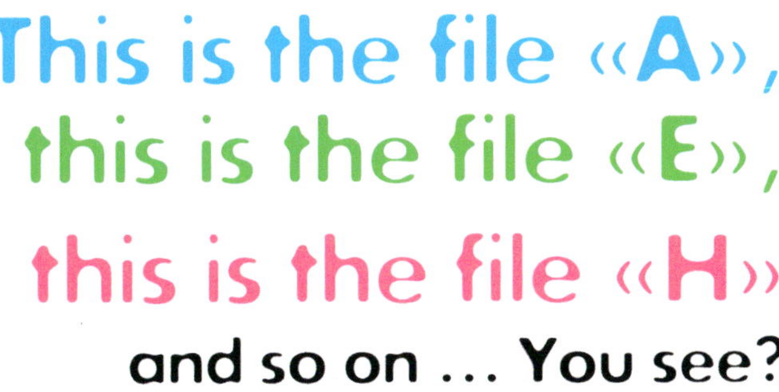

This is the file «A»,
this is the file «E»,
this is the file «H»

and so on … You see?

**Well done!**
Now let's see the numbers.

Our numbers are also here for a reason, they indicate the numbers of houses in which the pieces live. And also rank. For example,

the 1st rank,
the 4th rank
or the 8th,

and which one do you want to show?
A rank – row of squares from left to right.

# HELLO.
## Today I will tell you a story!
## And not just a fairy tale,
## but about a small,
## cheerful kitty!

Once upon a time there lived one small red kitty
and his name was Timoshka.
The kitty was very fond of 2 things: fish and making a visit.
And then one day he gathered to visit
«But can I go empty-handed?» – thought the kitty
and went to catch a fish at the nearest pond.
He caught a lot of fish. But while he was visiting,
his bag was torn and the fish scattered.
The fish were not simple and not just folded!
There were 16, each type of fish was 2.

## Help the kitty
## collect the same fish!

Let's take colored pencils or pens and draw a line from one fish
to another the same?!

And let's name them! Wow, how great you get!
And so we gathered all the fish and our
kitty safely arrived to visit. Where he treated another kitty!
You see how you helped him! Well done!

**And now a little more to solve!**

# TASKS. DOUBLE CHECK.
## PRACTICUM 2

So, today we are solving problems in 2 moves!
But do not be afraid, they are very easy!
You will not notice how you solve them!
First, find the black king
and touch him.
And now we find a white piece
that is looking at it.
Ok, yes, it's a rook!
And who is stopping the check from
being set by the rook to the king?
That's right, bishop.
How are we going?

**Answer:**

1.Bd8-f6 ++ (tell me, how many pieces attacked the king?
That's right, the check from 2 pieces is called  Double check!
The king moves away) … K h8-h7,
and now how do we checkmate the king?
Correctly!


2. Ra8-h8 #.
So today we have solved the task on the checkmate
in 2 moves with the help of a double check.
So, double check is a check from 2 pieces. Remember?
Well done. In writing, the check is indicated by +,
and if it is a double check, what do you think,
how many pluses will we write?
Yes, 2. ++ is a double check.

So who is looking at the king?
Right, rook, but who is interfere? That's right, bishop!
How do we get the bishop and rook to attack the king?

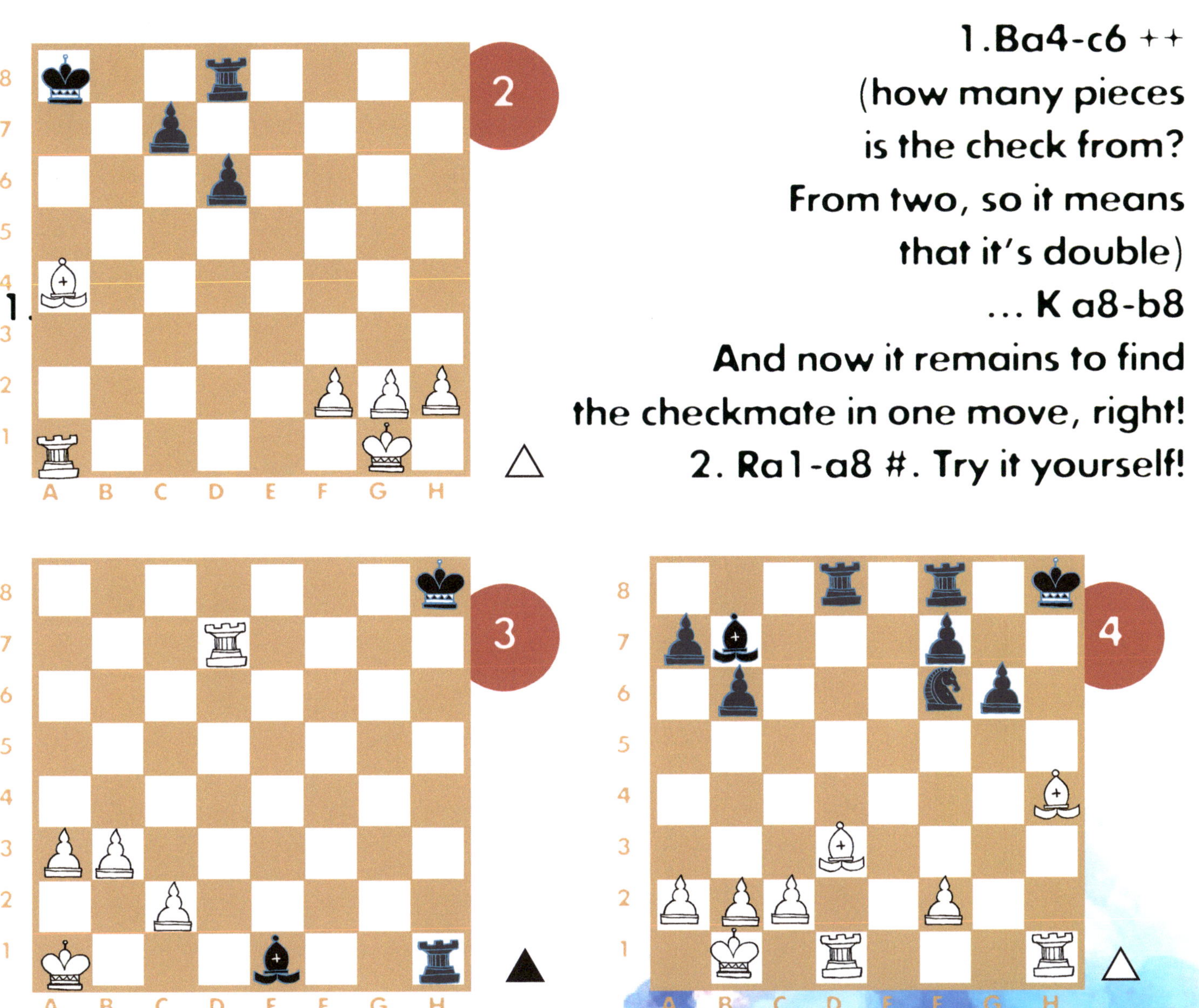

1.Ba4-c6 ++
(how many pieces
is the check from?
From two, so it means
that it's double)
... K a8-b8
And now it remains to find
the checkmate in one move, right!
2. Ra1-a8 #. Try it yourself!

Pay attention to the pawn that save the king, everywhere where
it is covered by pawns that are not in one row, weak squares
are formed, because the pawn has ceased to control them, so
it's very important not to move pawns from the king! Otherwise,

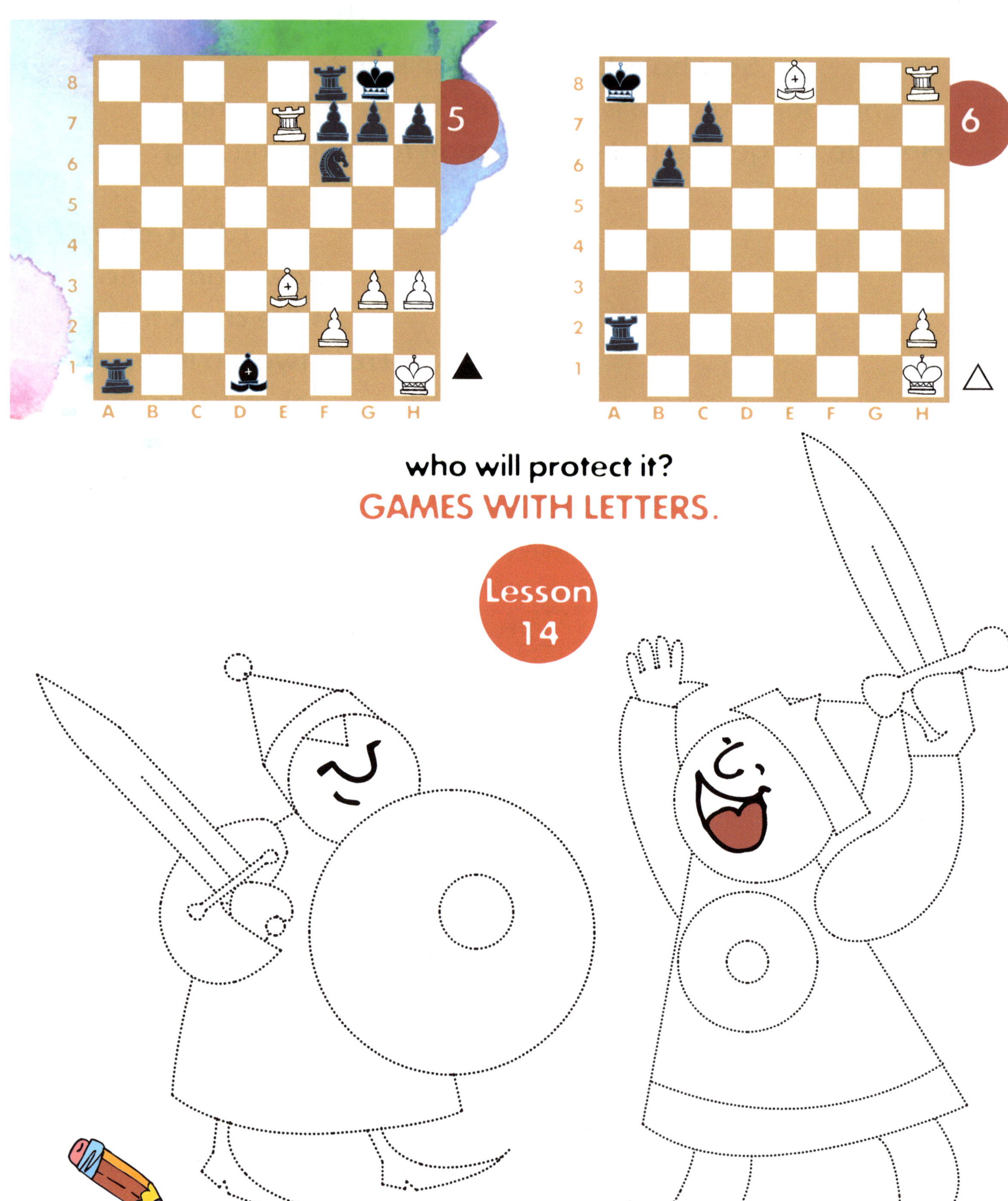



who will protect it?
# GAMES WITH LETTERS.

Lesson
14

Find a pair, draw the letters in different colors

And now two our kitties:
red and black decided to play hopscotch.
And before jumping, everyone should name
the letter that it is going to jump on.
Write the missing letters!

Let's call all the letters along with them,
and jump?! Fine.
You do it all!

# Spelling letters

Aa Aa Aa Aa Aa Aa Aa Aa Aa Aa Aa
Bb Bb Bb Bb Bb Bb Bb Bb Bb Bb Bb
Cc Cc Cc Cc Cc Cc Cc Cc Cc Cc Cc
Dd Dd Dd Dd Dd Dd Dd Dd Dd Dd Dd
Ee Ee Ee Ee Ee Ee Ee Ee Ee Ee Ee
Ff Ff Ff Ff Ff Ff Ff Ff Ff Ff Ff
Gg Gg Gg Gg Gg Gg Gg Gg Gg Gg Gg
Hh Hh Hh Hh Hh Hh Hh Hh Hh Hh Hh

## Find and draw the same pieces in the same colors.

# PIECES, DESIGNATIONS.

since chess is an international game, we will get to know some concepts and names of pieces in English.

 K - king

 Q - Queen

 B - Bishop

 K - Knight

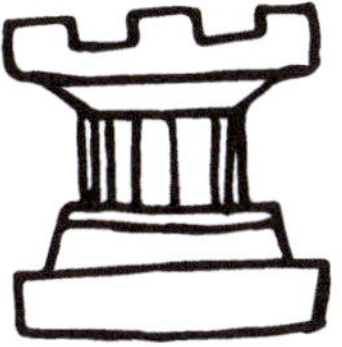 R - Rock

 pawn

Pawn is not a piece, therefore, when we write,
we do not denote it.
And in English it is called pawn.

**And now I will tell you more
about some important chess entries!**

: capture          # checkmate; mate.
+ check            ++ double check

# «PIN»

**Lesson 16**

Hello, today I'll tell you what a pinned piece is.
This is a piece that protects the king from the check and therefore cannot move anywhere.

**1** We call such a piece pinned, and all 3 pieces together we call «Pin». In this case, the knight cannot move anywhere. Because the king has a check. A knight is a pinned piece, and all pieces together are a pin.

Remember, this is very important! If the opponent tries to move a pinned piece with you in the game, you must tell him: «An impossible move, the check is opened to the king!» He must make another (possible move after that). If the dispute could not be resolved, it is necessary to call an arbiter.

So, tasks on the topic «Pin».

**2** How to attack the king?
Correct: Rc1-c8 #
And what do you think: Na7: c8?
No, because the knight covers the king from the check, so such a knight is called pinned, and all together a pin.
**W**ell done, you understand everything.

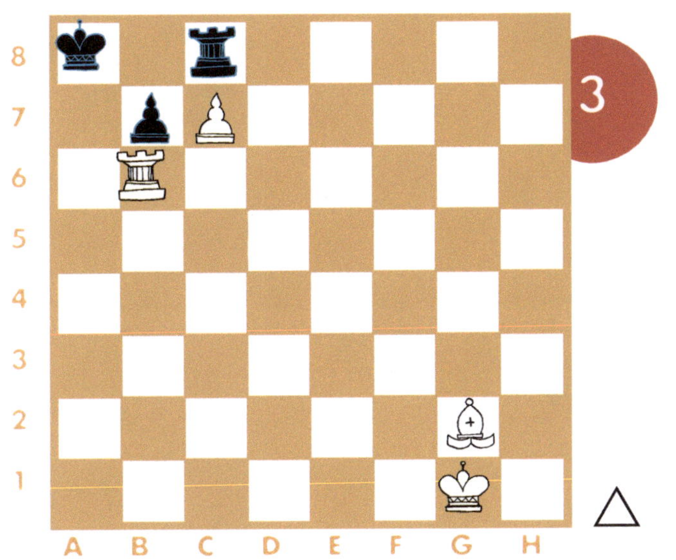

You understood correctly:
1. Rb6: a6 #.
Why can't a pawn with b7:
on a6?
That's right, because the king
will have a check from the bishop.

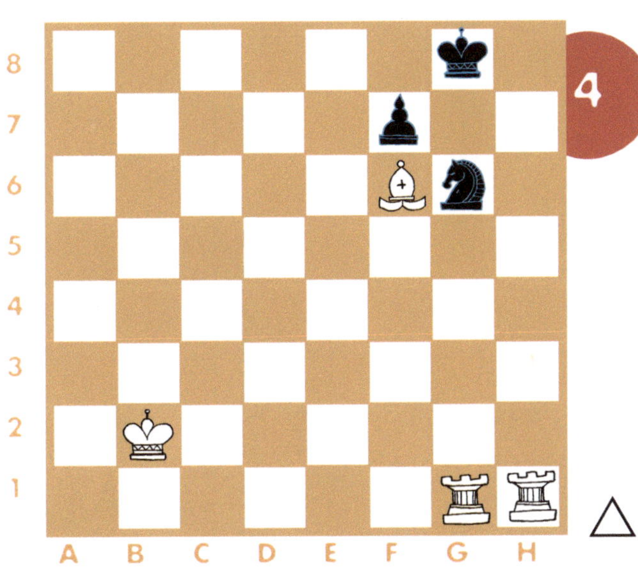

Who will attack the king?
That's right, rook! 1. Rh1-h8 #.
Can a knight beat your rook?
No, it cannot because
the check opens from the rook.
According to the rules of chess,
a king cannot remain
under the check.

# PIN. PRACTICUM 3.

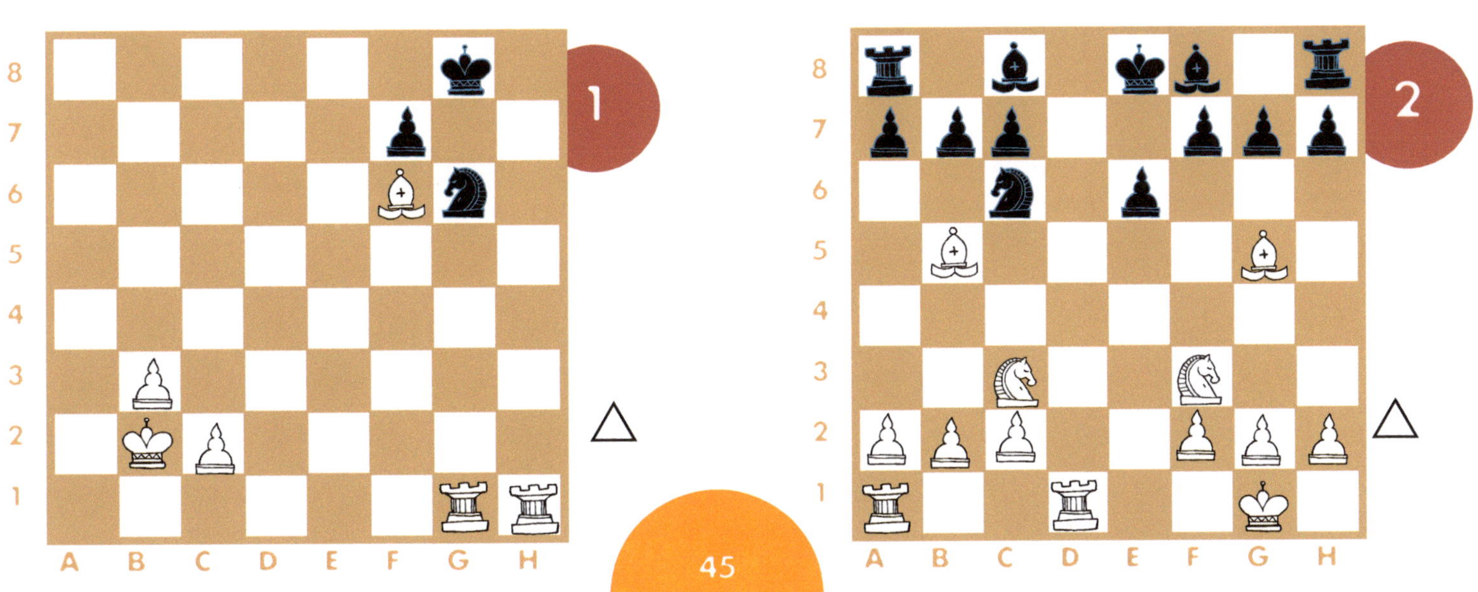

# The answers

(1) 1. Rh1-h8 #
a related piece here is Ng6.
Therefore, such a knight cannot leave. (2) 1. Rd1-d8 # Why is a knight with c6 unable to beat the rook on d8? That's right, because it's pinned! (3) 1. Ra1-a8 # right! What is the pinned piece here? Nb6! Fine! (4) 1. ... Rc8-c1 # Why can't Na2 beat the rook on c1? That's right, because it is pinned, it was pinned by Rook on a8. (5) 1. ... Rf8-f1 #. (6) 1. Rf1-f8 # what is the pinned piece here? That's right, Bg7. Who pinned it? Right, Bb2. (7) 1. ... Rc8-c1 # What is the pinned piece here? Yes, bishop on b2. (8) 1. Re8-e1 #
What is the pinned piece in this task? That's right, knight f3..

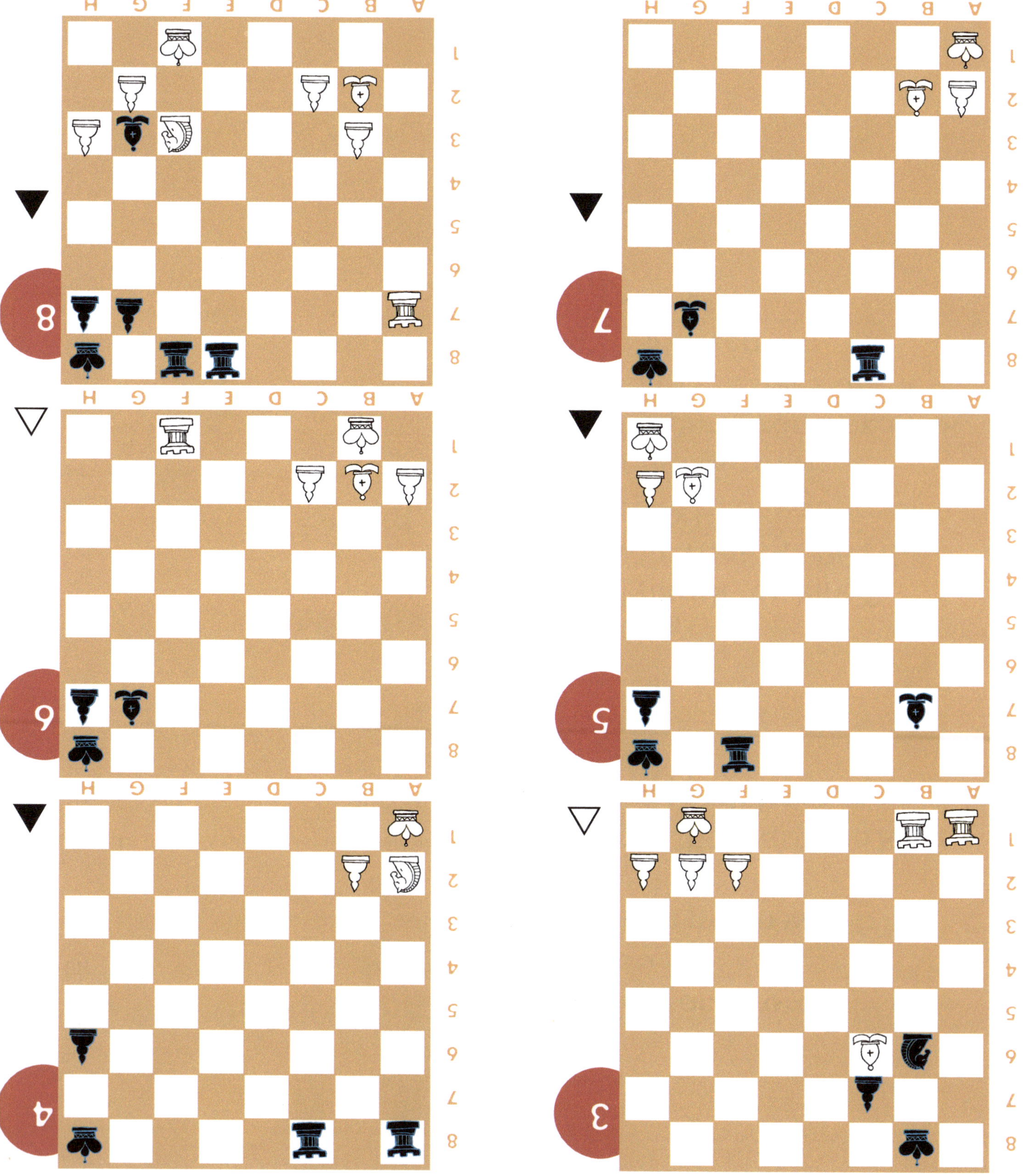

# COST
# OF THE PIECES

Hello, today I will tell you about the cost of the pieces, or rather: which of them is the strongest and in what we measure it? And we will measure it in sweets! Can you imagine?

**The queen costs 9 candies,**

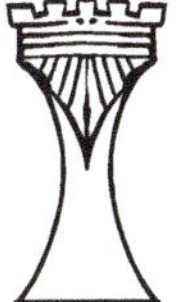

**Rook 5 candies,**

**Bishop 3 candies,**

**Knight 3 candies,**

**Pawn – 1**

So, the more candies, the stronger the piece, the stronger the piece you eat, the more candies you have. Here is such arithmetic!

# CHECKMATE IN 1 MOVE.
## PAWN PROMOTION.

Let's see, the white pawn
moved far?
Right, far away, how much
is it left before promotion?
That's right, one move!
Who can it turn into,
so that the king has an attack:
right in the queen!
1.c7-c8Q #.

**Well done,
you solved the first task!**

**And try the rest yourself!**

1.F7-f8Q#.

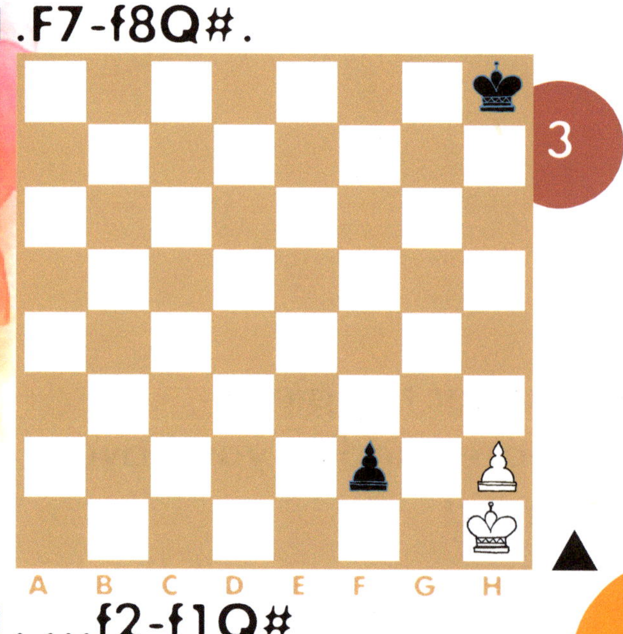

1. ...f2-f1Q#

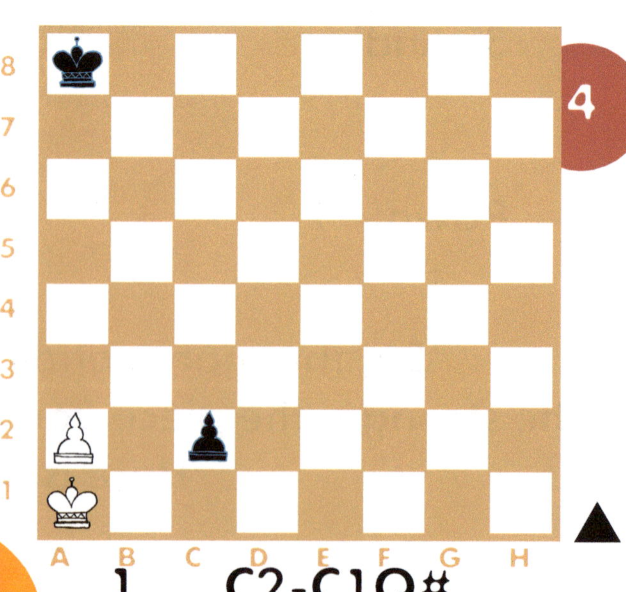

1. ...C2-C1Q#.

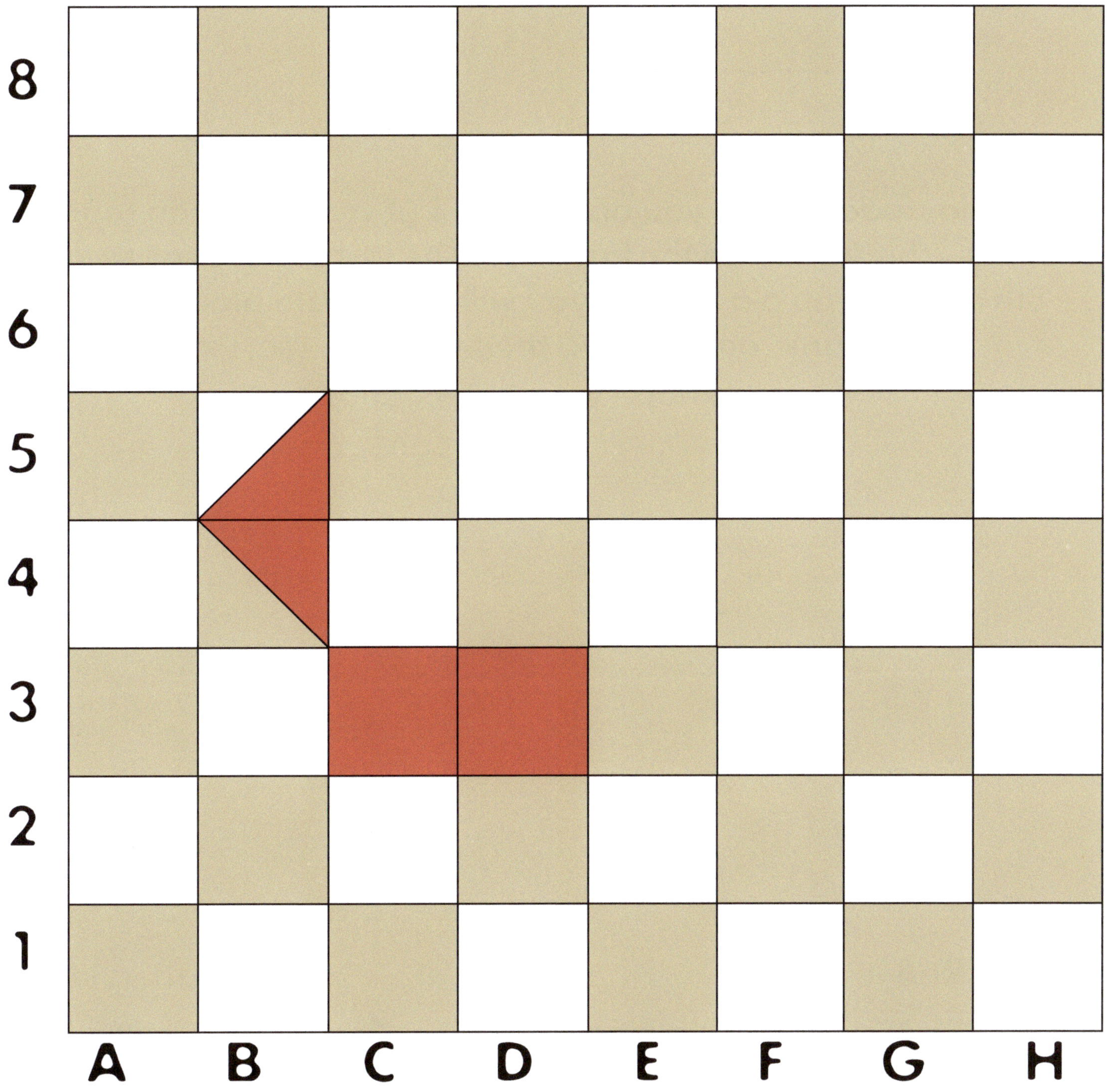

## Color these squares and see what piece you get.

B1, C1, D1, E1
E2◣, D2, C2, B2◢
C3, D3
B4◥, C4, D4, E4◤
E5◣, D5, C5, B5◢
C6, D6

Lesson 19

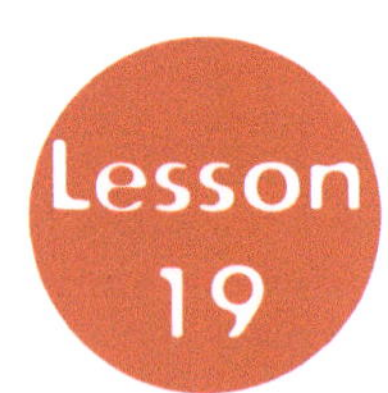

# «LUFT»

## CHECKMATE ON THE LAST LINE.

Hello, today I'll tell you one simple but very common topic in chess: «checkmate on the last line». The last line we call the 1st or 8th rank. If you play white, you will checkmate black on the 8th rank, and if black, then white on the 1st.

I hope you understand!

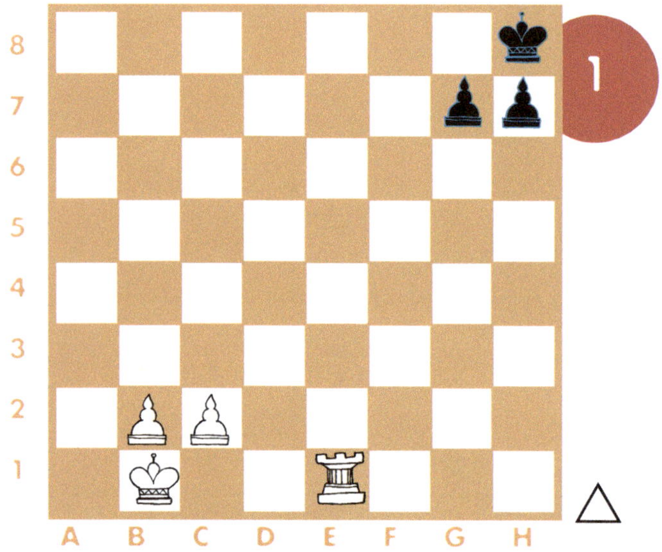


1. ... Re8-e1#

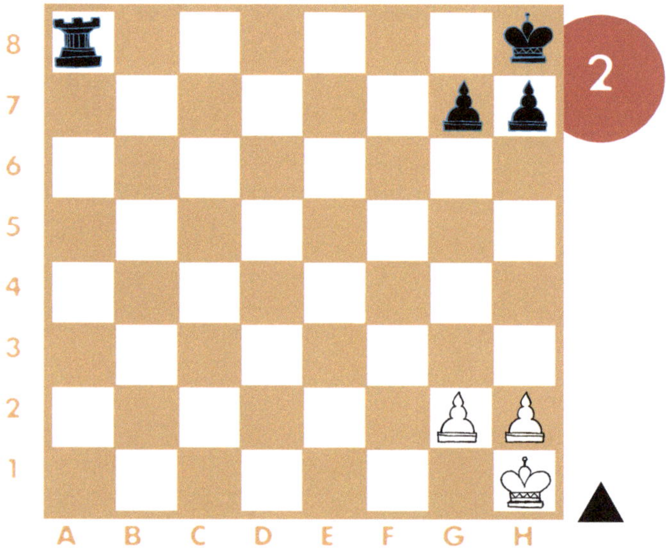


1. ...Ra8-a1#

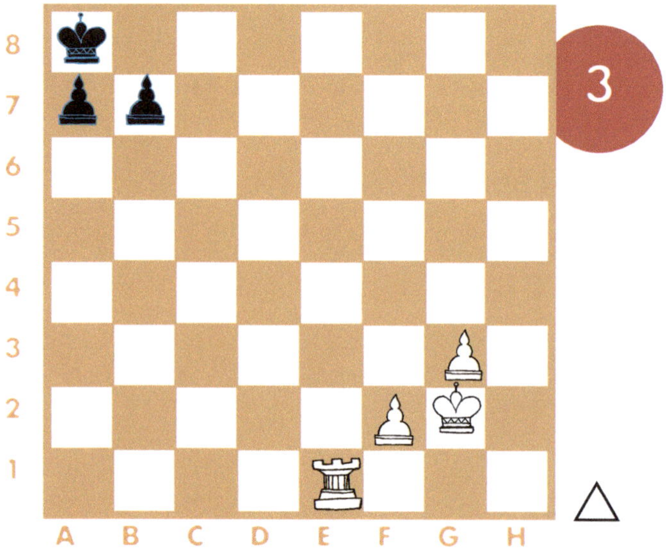


1. Re1-e8#

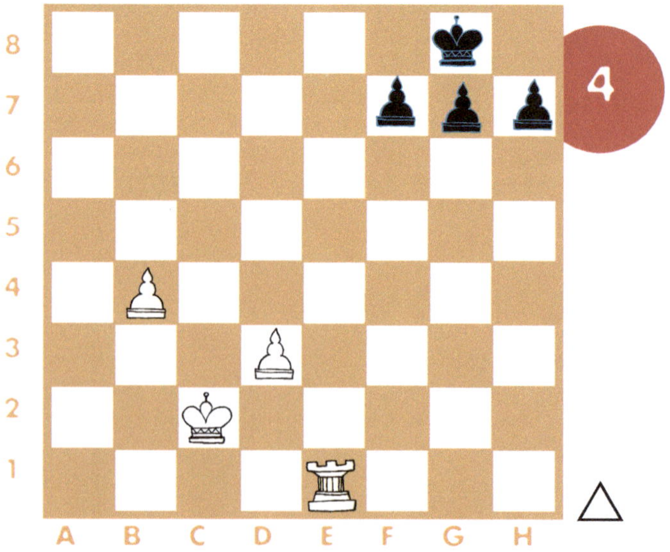


1. Re1-e8#

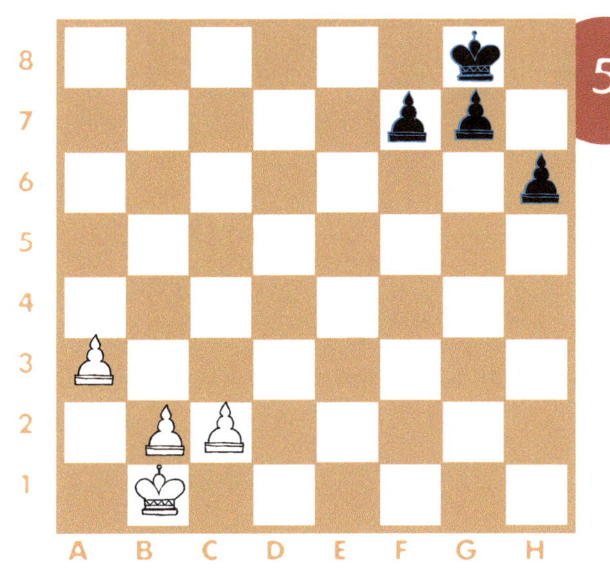

So, today you learned how to checkmate on the last line. As you can see, it's easy!

And I'll tell you a little secret:
to avoid such a checkmate, you can slightly push the last (near the edge of the chessboard) pawn by one square after castling, then the king will be able to «escape» after the attack.

**And such a position in a pawn structure is called a «luft» in chess.**

# CONTENT: